Sacred Windows: Drawing and Seeing

(in the Sacred Colors Series)

Christopher L. Smith

ISBN: 0-9985295-0-8
ISBN-13: 978-0-9985295-0-9

DEDICATION

This book is dedicated to those who will color it. It is my prayer that as you color it, you will be able to have time in prayer, connecting to God in the same way that people have throughout the ages in some of these sacred spaces.

This book, the first in a series, is also dedicated to those who have fostered my interest in combining my faith with my interest in mathematics. Special thanks is given to those who allowed me to explore sacred geometry both at Yale Divinity School (and the Institute of Sacred Music and Berkeley Divinity School) and the Sacred Geometry Library at Saint John the Divine Cathedral in New York City.

CONTENTS

ACKNOWLEDGMENTS

Appreciation is given to those who have photographed these sacred spaces and allowed others to use these images. Credit for the original photographs are provided on the pages that show how the window exists on the reverse of the coloring page.

INTRODUCTION

This book is a little different than other books that you might have used. It is really a hybrid of a coloring book, a journal and a spiritual resource. This is done to allow you to interface with the sacred in a variety of ways.

In this book you will have an opportunity to go to eight different sacred spaces and explore a window that is there. When you first turn to the pages of that space, you will be presented with a coloring page for that sacred window. Your coloring on that page will allow you to express your own response to the window. Following this page, you will find a page that includes a picture of the window as it appears in that space along with a brief description about both the space and why this was included in this particular book. Also included in this description will generally be a couple of things that you may want to consider and think about. On the third page for each sacred window will be another coloring page of that window. As you use that page, you are encouraged to think about the information that was presented as well as what it is like to color it knowing more of the context. The final page for each sacred window is a journal page for you to be able to record what is happening to you related to this sacred window: your thoughts, your prayers, your emotions, your responses, etc.

It is my prayer that you will be able to deepen your faith, even a little, as you engage in these activities. I also believe that you may be able to gain from using this book even if you chose to only do part of the activities. It is okay if you are someone who is more focused on coloring books or more focused on journaling or even who just want to know a little more about some sacred windows. Use this resource in the way that you feel will be helpful in your journey.

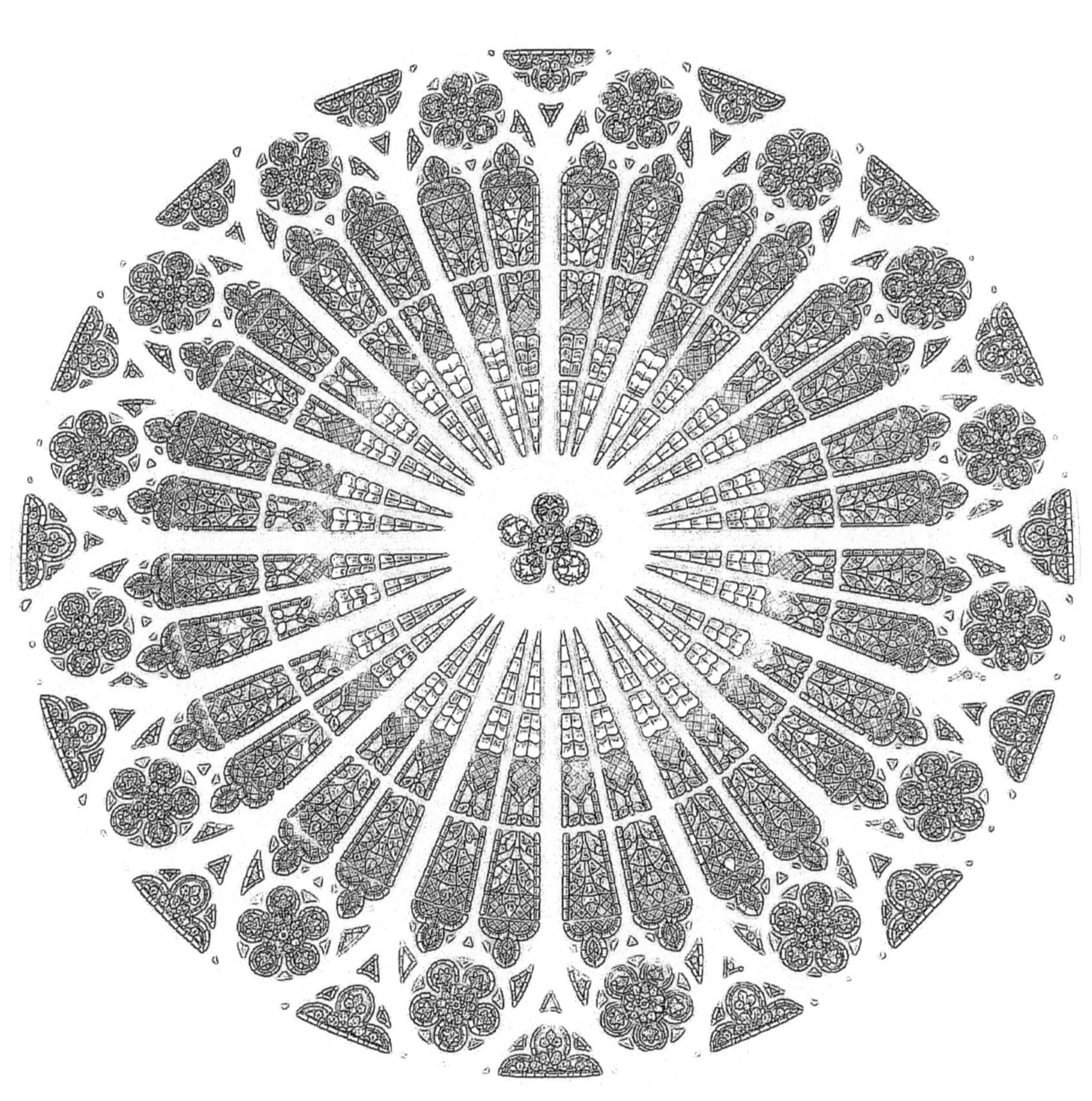

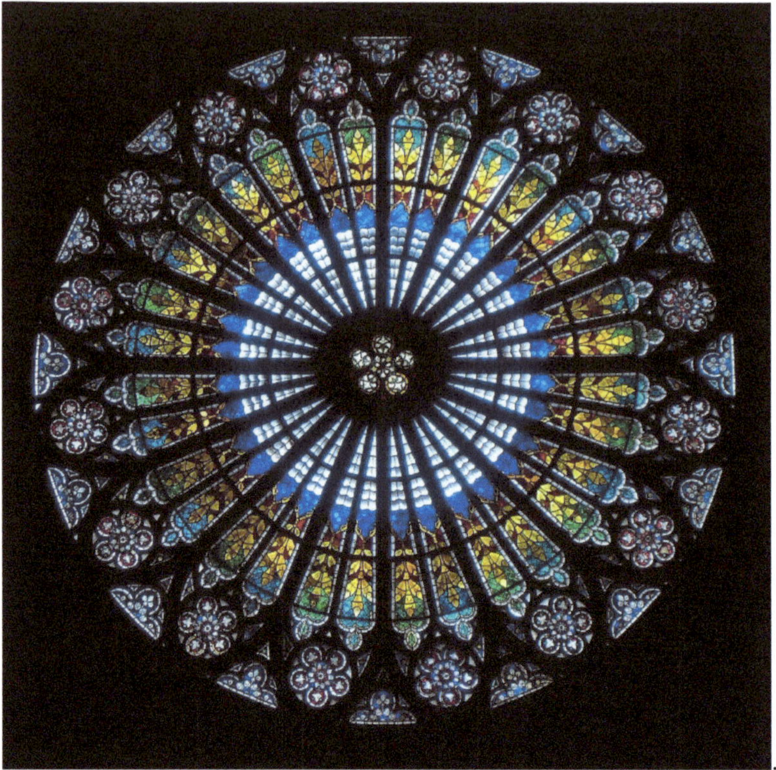

Interior of the rose at Strasbourg Cathedral. Clostridium, 2008, Public Domain

The Cathedrale Notre-Dame de Strasbourgh (also known as the Cathedral of our Lady of Strasbourgh or Strasbourgh Minster) has a lot of unique characteristics as a sacred site. For over two centuries it was the world's tallest building (and is still the sixth tallest church in the world) because of the height of its tower built in the Middle Ages. For its time, the fact that it only has one tower is also unique, even though the original plan was to build a sister tower. This building has also served as a Roman Catholic cathedral and as a Protestant church during the Reformation. In this way the grandness of this window fits in within this building. As is typical for many older cathedrals, it was built over a long timeframe. It also was built on the site of previous churches and religious buildings, going back to a temple during Roman times.

This sacred window is a good example of a rose window. Rose windows are generally circular and have an underlying symmetric structure. This window is based entirely on geometric shapes and includes no pictures. Some rose windows will include depictions of people associated with that church building or with God's people throughout the ages, but the absence of this does not mean that theological statements are not being made by the patterns that are within the way the window is constructed.

As you work with this rose window, think about ways that beauty contributes to your spiritual walk. Think about ways that you can find subtle messages being conveyed through the patterns and the subtleties of aspects of the window. How can you add to these messages in the way that you add color to the window?

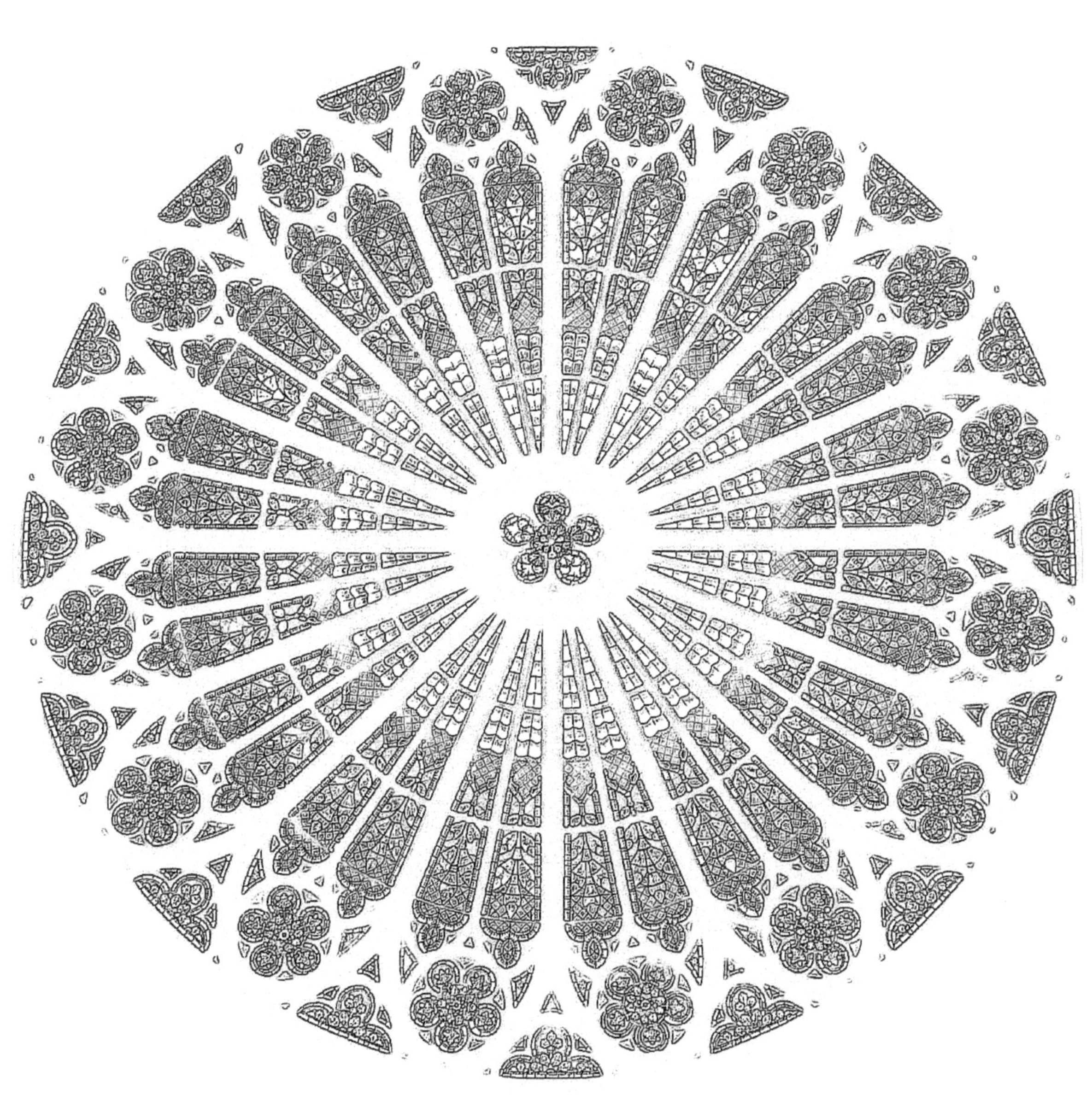

REFLECTION ON COLORING THIS SACRED WINDOW

Use this space to record some of the thoughts from your coloring of this sacred window. These reflections could be about the particular window or be thoughts that you had while coloring.

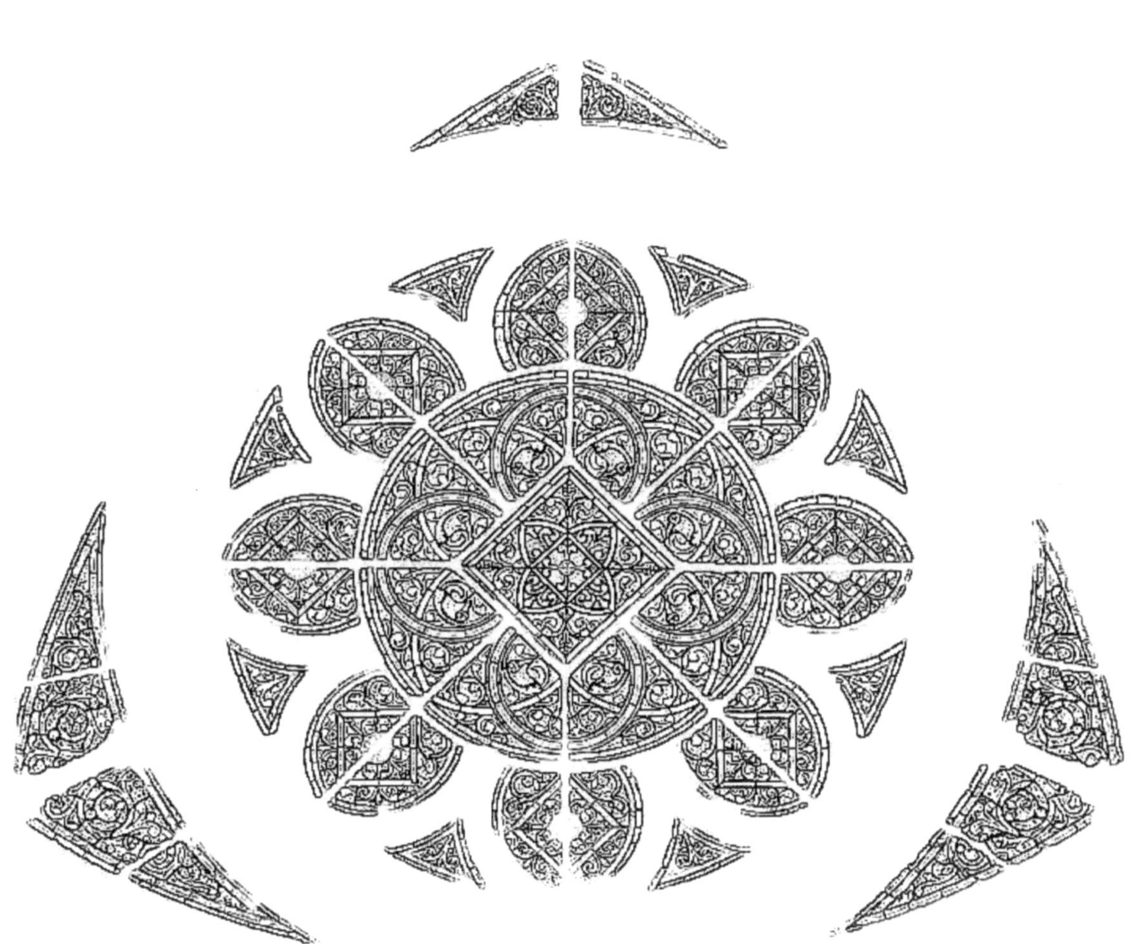

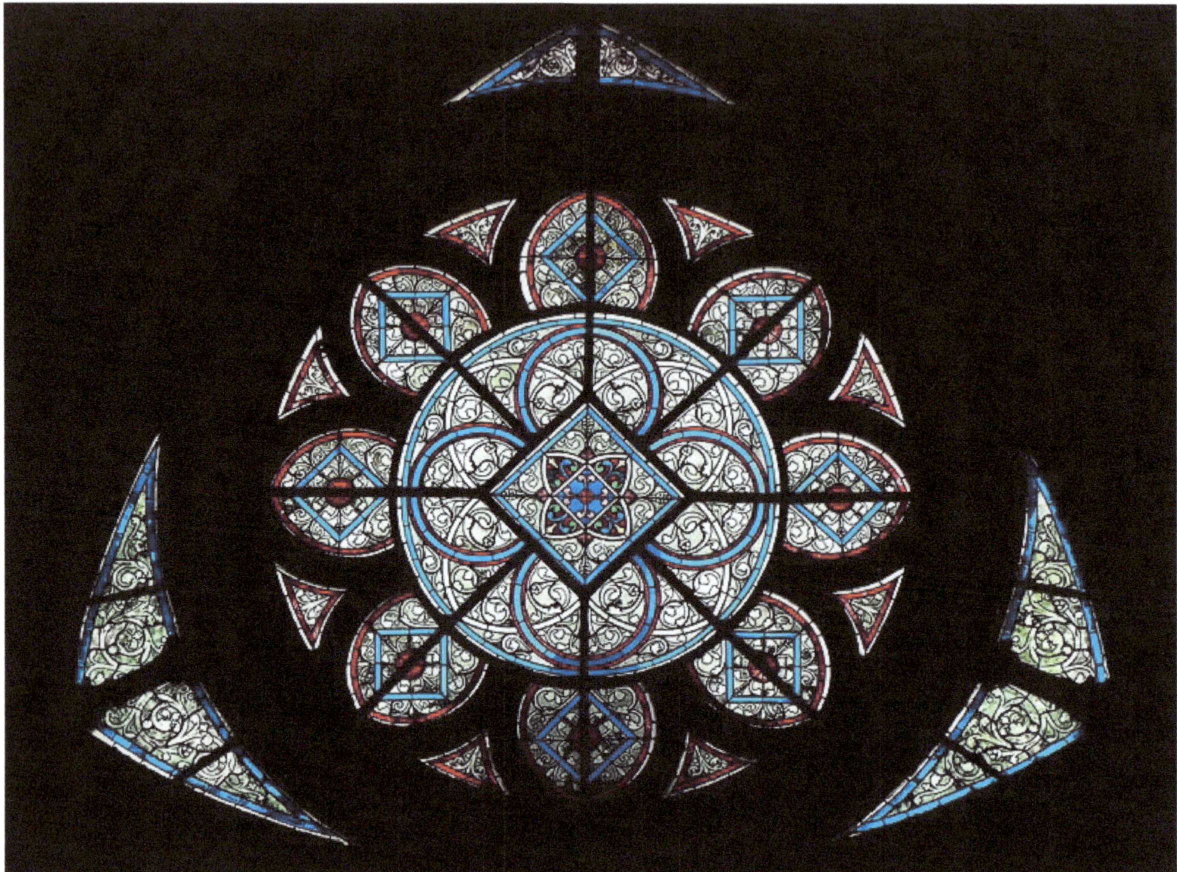

Stained glass windows of Amiens Cathedral, pic-013. Alfvanbeem, 2013, Public Domain.

Amiens Cathedral (or more formally the Cathedral Basilica of Our Lady of Amiens) is a Roman Catholic cathedral in the Picardy section of France, north of Paris. It is among the largest churches in the world and the tallest complete cathedral in France. While it was built in the thirteenth century, its glass is all not original. This is in part due to the number of disasters and destructions that this cathedral has suffered.

While the cathedral has more colorful stained glass windows, including a great rose window, this window was selected because of its variety of symmetry. While the central symmetry is based on a four-part symmetry, which is echoed elsewhere in the architectural design of this cathedral, the window encloses this in a tri-fold symmetry.

It is quite possible that you will have opted to color in the parts that are clear glass in reality. This would probably create a more attractive design but would also have run counter to the purpose of the window and that was to bring in light into the large interior space of this cathedral. In what ways do you allow light to shine into your own space and in what ways do you provide things that look good on the surface but yet affect what you are being given to see by?

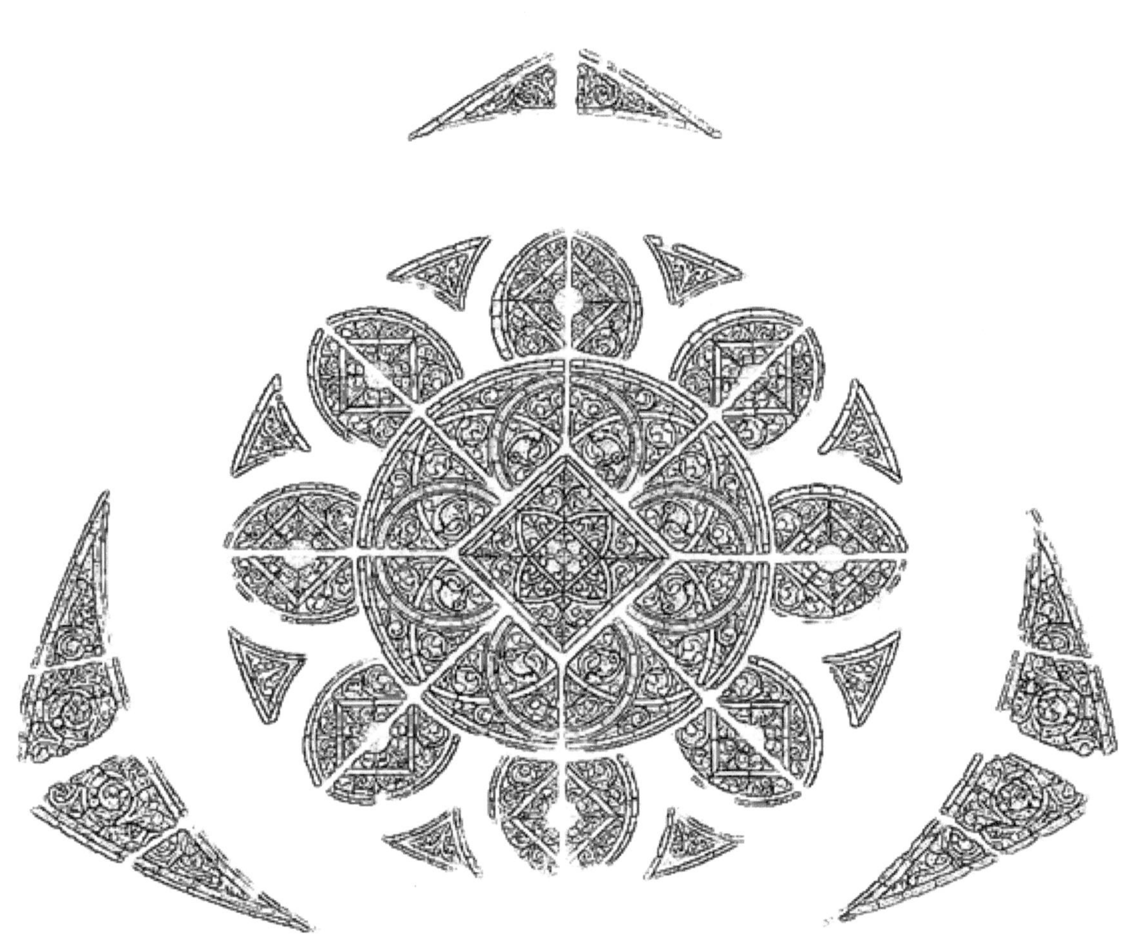

REFLECTION ON COLORING THIS SACRED WINDOW

Use this space to record some of the thoughts from your coloring of this sacred window. These reflections could be about the particular window or be thoughts that you had while coloring.

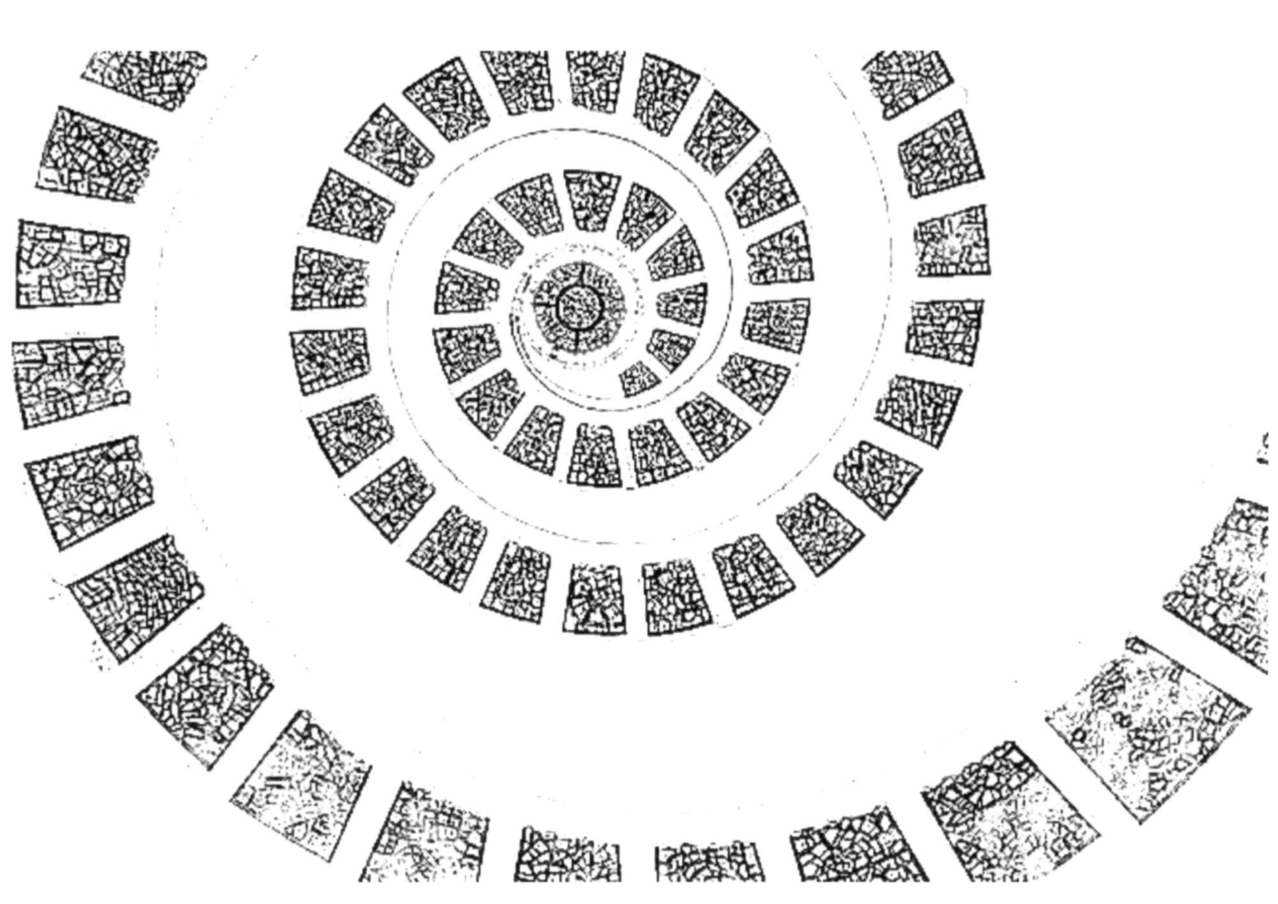

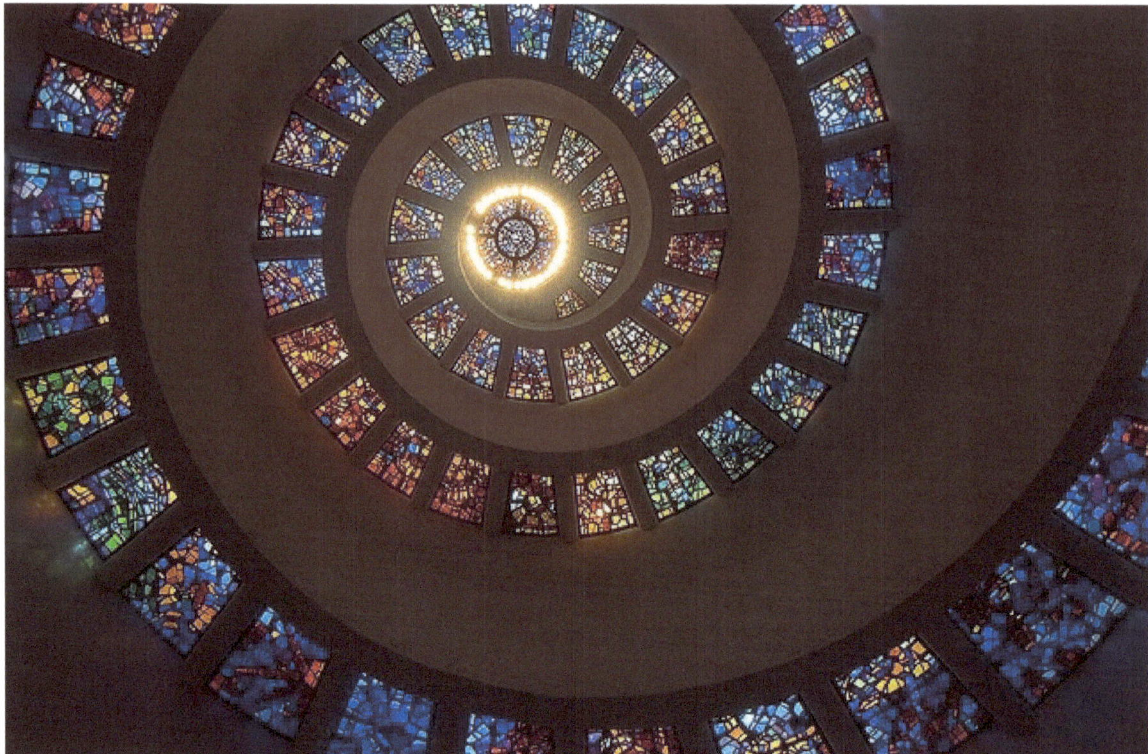

Thanksgiving Square Chapel From the Floor. John McStravick, Creative Commons

The Chapel of Thanksgiving is part of Thanks-Giving Square in Dallas, Texas. It is the spiritual center of the square and was designed to be inclusive of people from a variety of faiths. Constructed in 1964, the entire Square utilizes influences from a variety of religious traditions and forms. The Chapel built in 1976 is inspired by the Great Mosque in Samarra, Iraq and draws on the spiral of life that follows mathematical patterns found in a diversity of religious traditions.

While the Square itself is sunken below the level of the earth in order to protect those there from the distractions of the world around them, the chapel spirals to a level ninety feet above street level. In contrast to the great cathedrals that house many of the stained glass windows in this collection, the chapel is a small spiral tower intended to be a place for people to offer prayers of thanks. The stained glass is at the top of the spire and is one of the largest horizontally mounted pieces of stained glass in the world and consists of 73 panels of stained glass.

When you look carefully at the design of the entire piece, you will notice that the coloring of the glass moves from darker on the outside to bright light at the center. Did you sense a similar movement as you colored this design? Did you feel a natural movement of the spiral that conforms to a pattern that is seen repeatedly in nature?

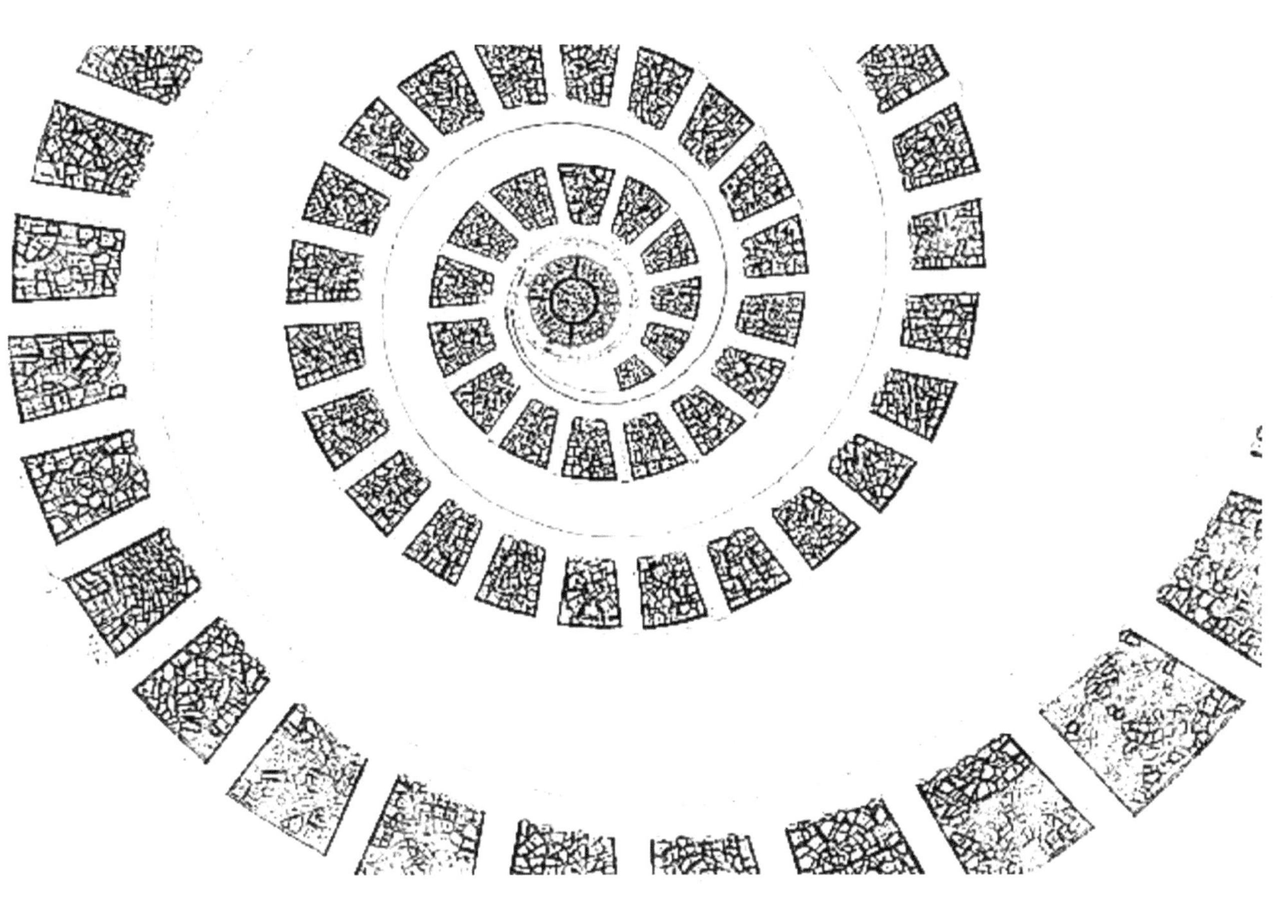

REFLECTION ON COLORING THIS SACRED WINDOW

Use this space to record some of the thoughts from your coloring of this sacred window. These reflections could be about the particular window or be thoughts that you had while coloring.

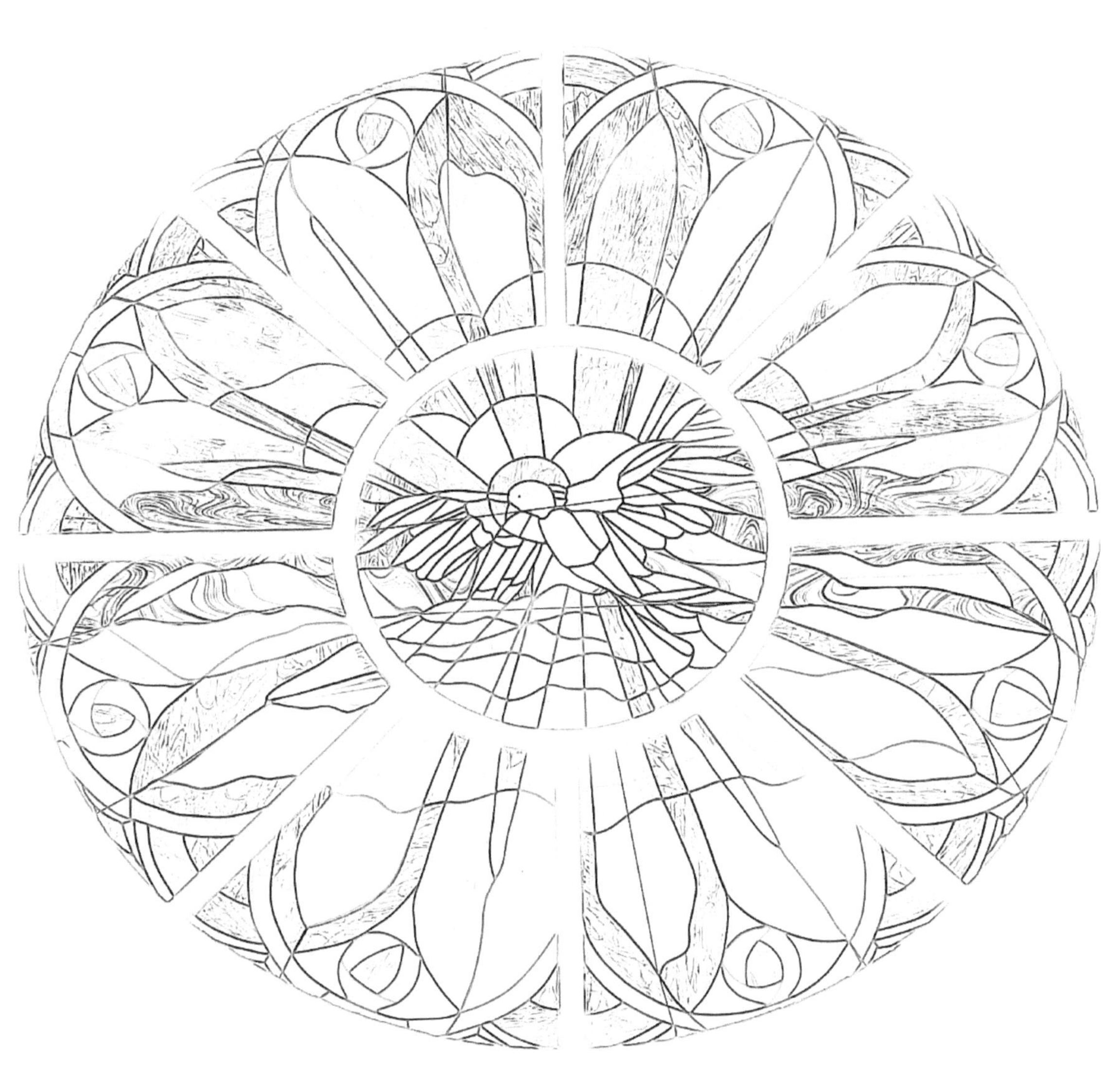

.

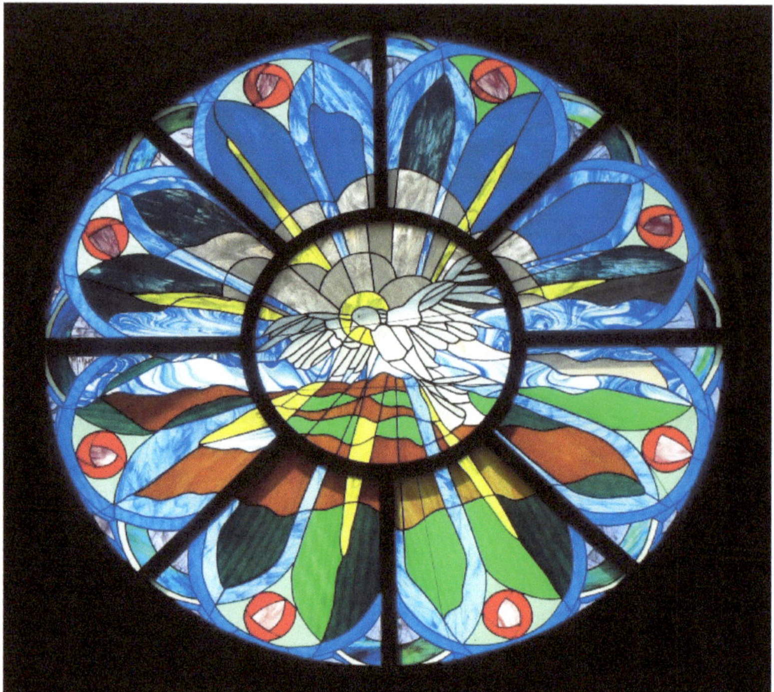

Saint John Neumann Church (Sunbury, Ohio) – stained glass, Holy Spirit rose window. Nheyob, 2013, Creative Commons.

While great works of stained glass are often thought to be part of great buildings like cathedrals, great examples are also found in more humble of spaces. The previous window came from a chapel in the public sphere and this window comes from a rural church in the United States.

Saint John Neumann is a parish that grew up out of the corn fields in the 1970s, growing quickly under the leadership of their founding pastor and a nun serving as pastoral assistant. The people of the area realized that they were in deed the church. Things worked so well in this parish that by the beginning of this century, the parish had outgrown its current space and again in 2013 the new church was expanded to double its size to create symmetry and enhanced beauty.

While many stained glass windows consist of pains of uniformly colored glass separated by pieces of metal, this example includes an example of where texturing is added by the way that individual pieces of glass are colored and shaded. This particular rose window can be found high above the altar in the worship space. The glow of the light through it serves as a reminder of the blowing of the Holy Spirit, as represented by the dove, to touch the hearts of the people. The central symbol of this rose window is also found in many sacred windows.

As you work on this particular window, in what ways have you seen God in more simple of spaces and ways? What role would you offer for the Holy Spirit in your own journey of faith? in the community that has been called together around you? What surrounds the Holy Spirit in the telling of your story?

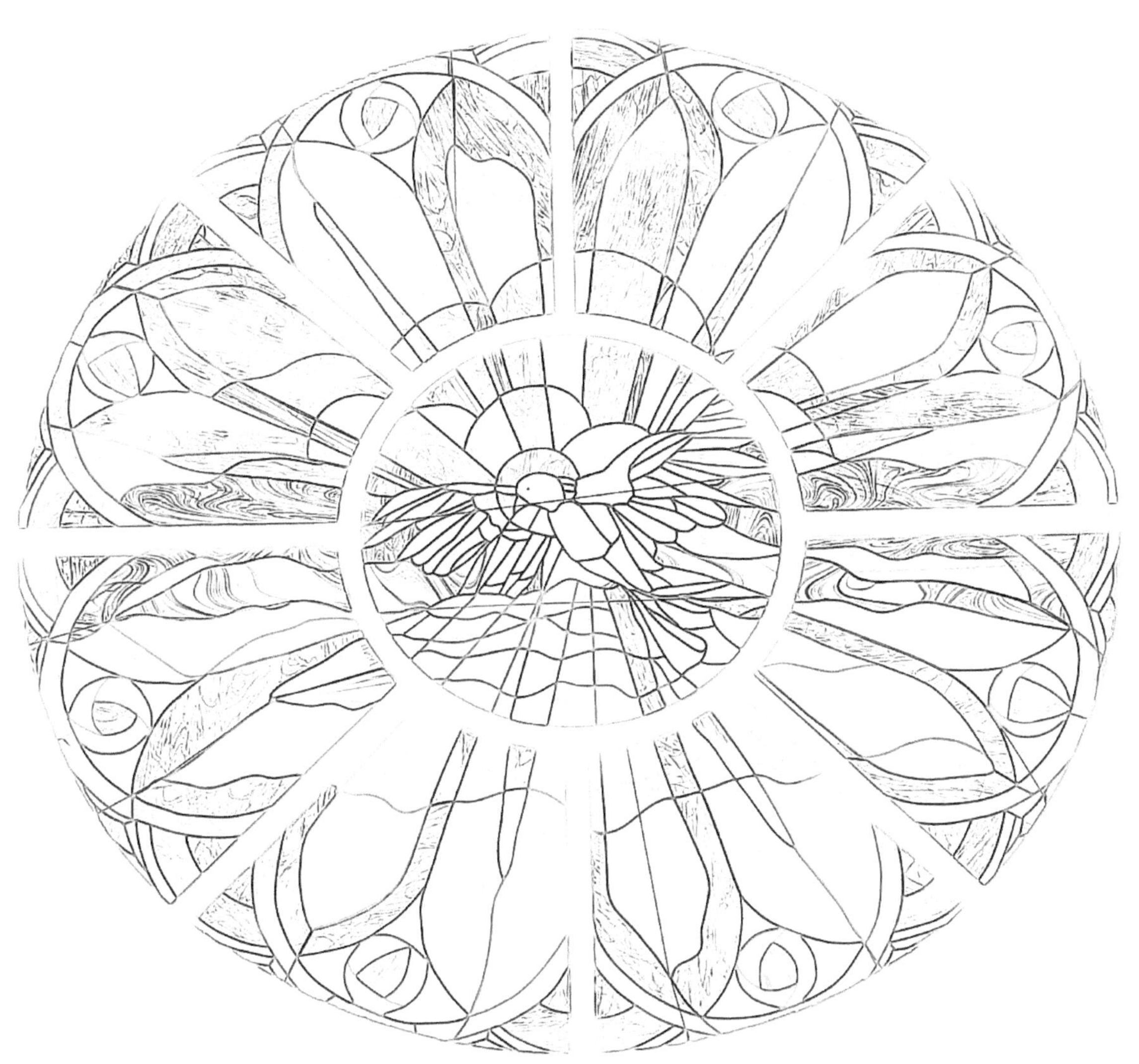

REFLECTION ON COLORING THIS SACRED WINDOW

Use this space to record some of the thoughts from your coloring of this sacred window. These reflections could be about the particular window or be thoughts that you had while coloring.

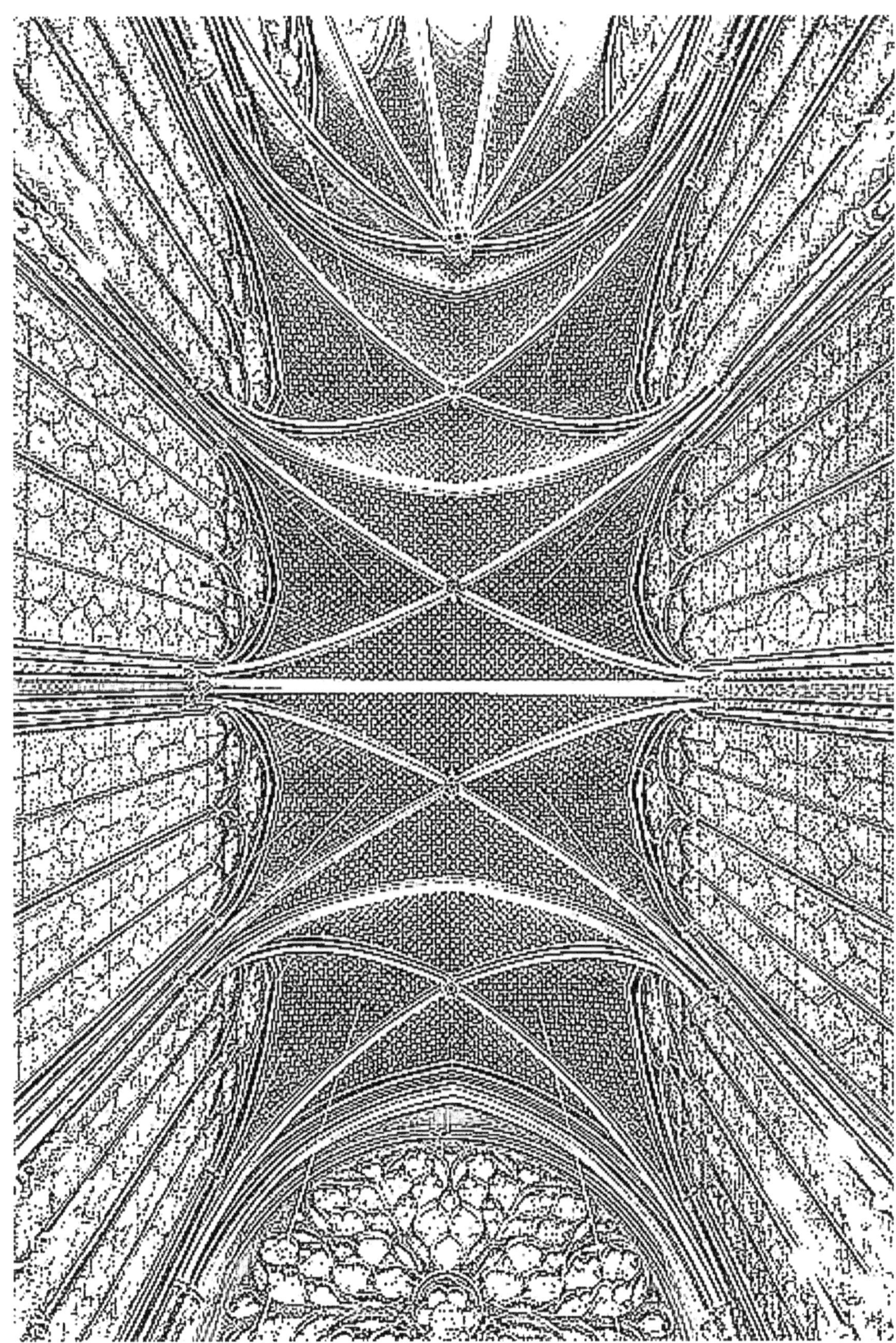

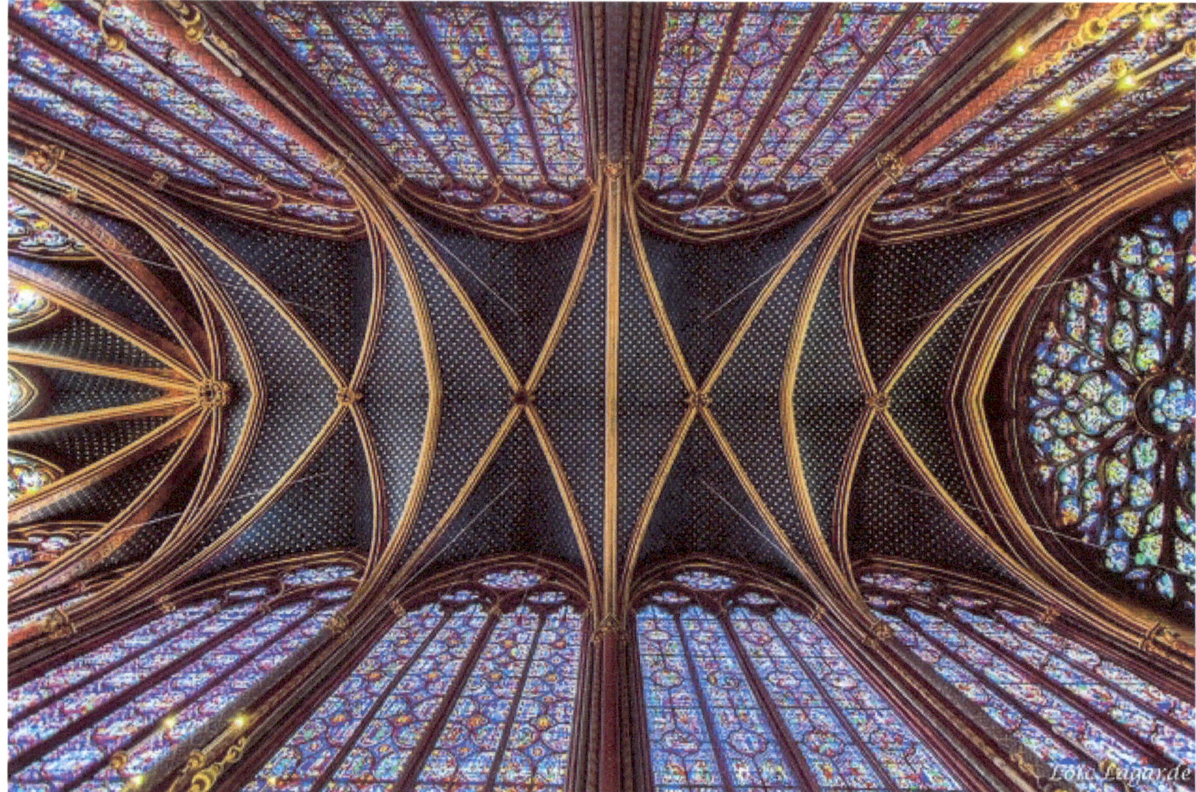

Saint Chapelle in Paris, France. Photo Credit: Loïc Lagarde, Creative Commons.

Saint Chapelle was impressively built in seven years in order to house precious Christian relics (including Christ's crown of thorns) that had been acquired by King Louis (later Saint Louis). It was consecrated in 1248. In translation, the name of this place translates as Holy Chapel and is a royal chapel in the Gothic style. It is found within the medieval Palais de la Cité within the main part of Paris, France. The palace was the residence of the Kings of France until the 14th century. It was damaged during the French Revolution but has gone through several renovations.

It is being included in this collection because of the extensive use of stained glass. In fact, Saint Chapelle is one of the most extensive collections of 13th century stained glass anywhere in the world. The stained glass is arranged into fifteen windows, each fifteen meters high. Together the panes depict 1,113 scenes from the Old and New Testaments recounting the history of the world until the arrival of the relics in Paris. From this view, you can tell that the masonry of the church is there simply to hold the stained glass, in contrast to other buildings that have significant amounts of masonry in between the windows.

This view is of the vaulted ceiling with the stained glass all around the outer edge. It helps to remind us that there is greatness in God's kingdom and that within the confines of holy space we are able to see how God has been active throughout history all around us.

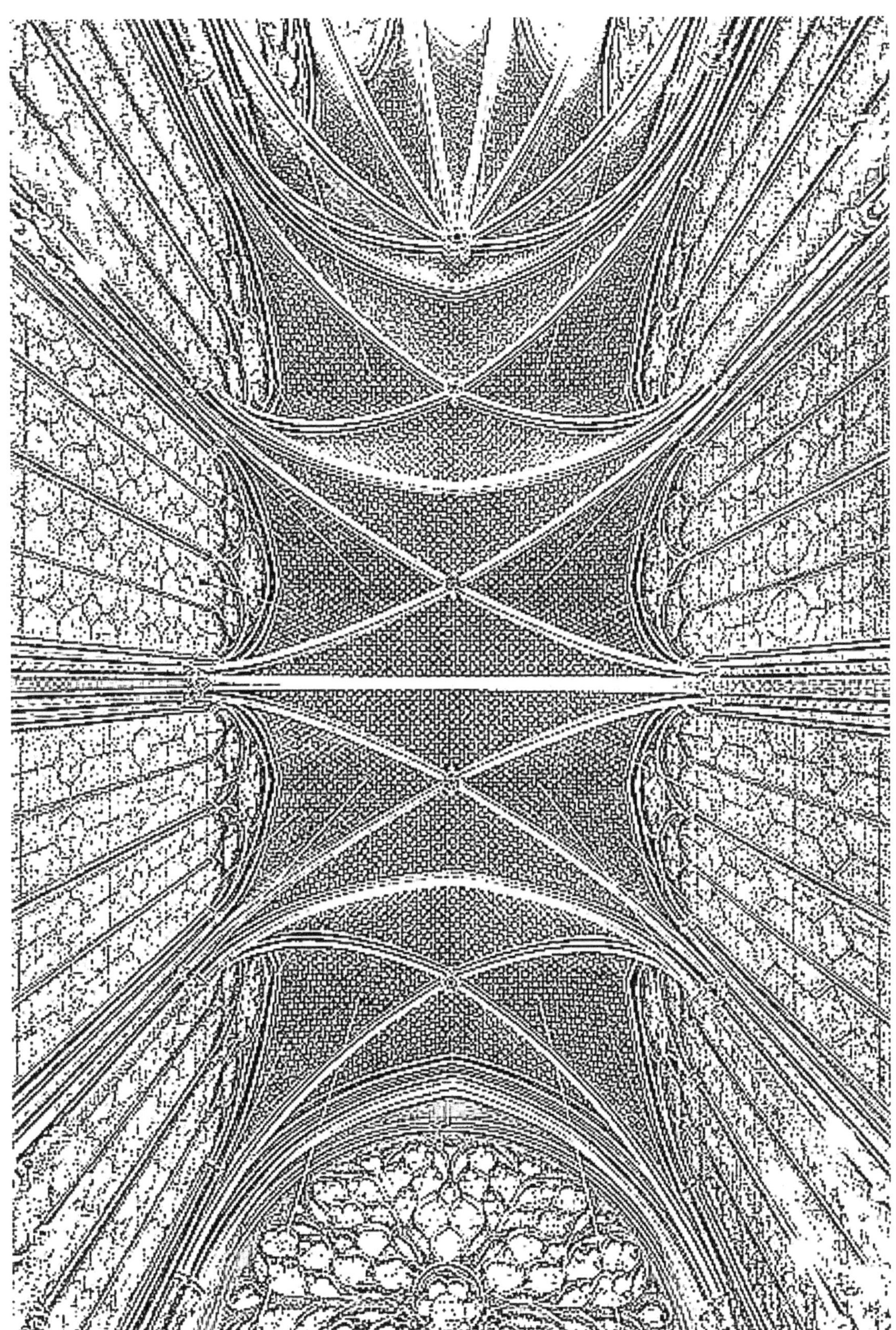

REFLECTION ON COLORING THIS SACRED WINDOW

Use this space to record some of the thoughts from your coloring of this sacred window. These reflections could be about the particular window or be thoughts that you had while coloring.

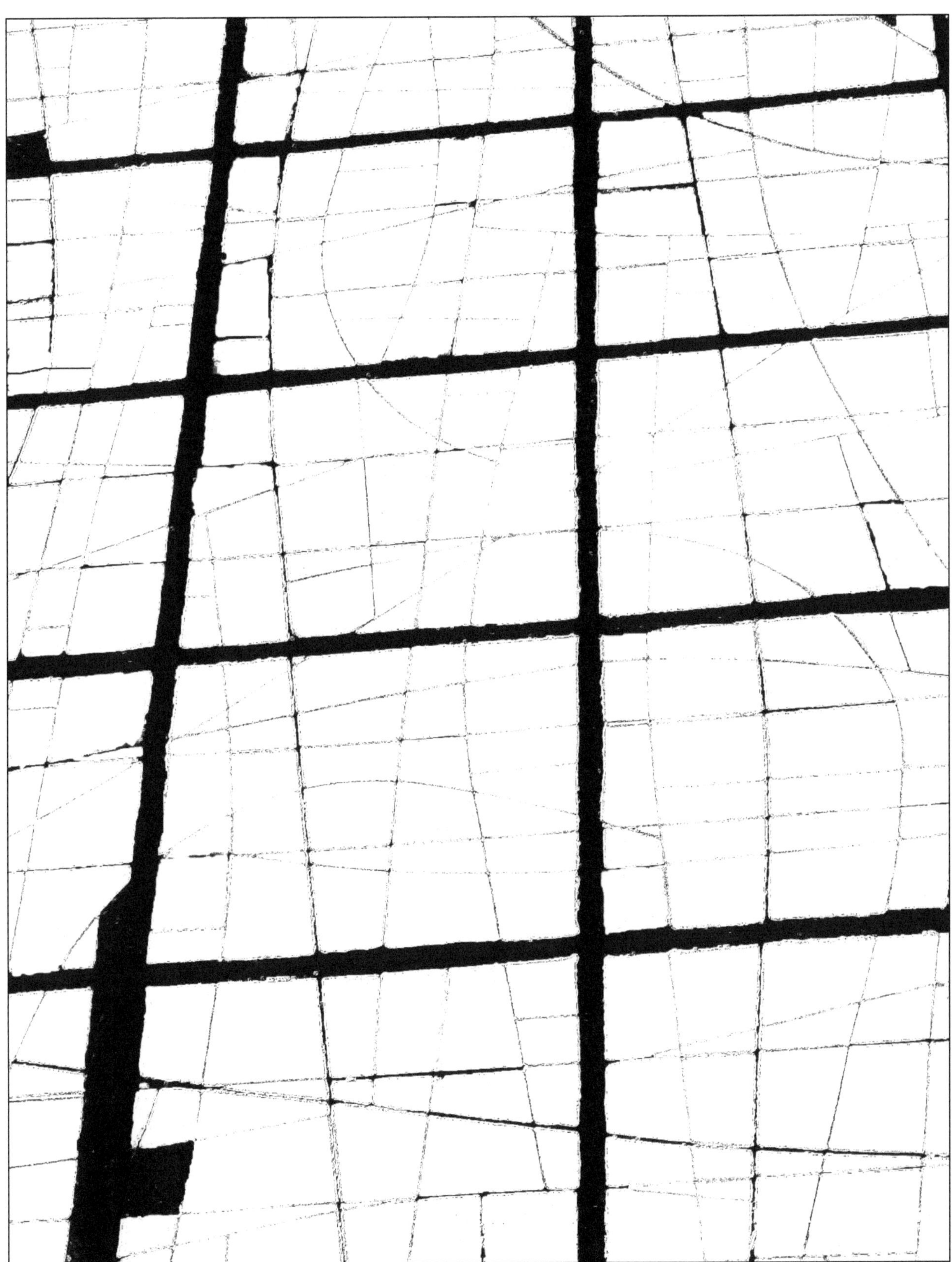

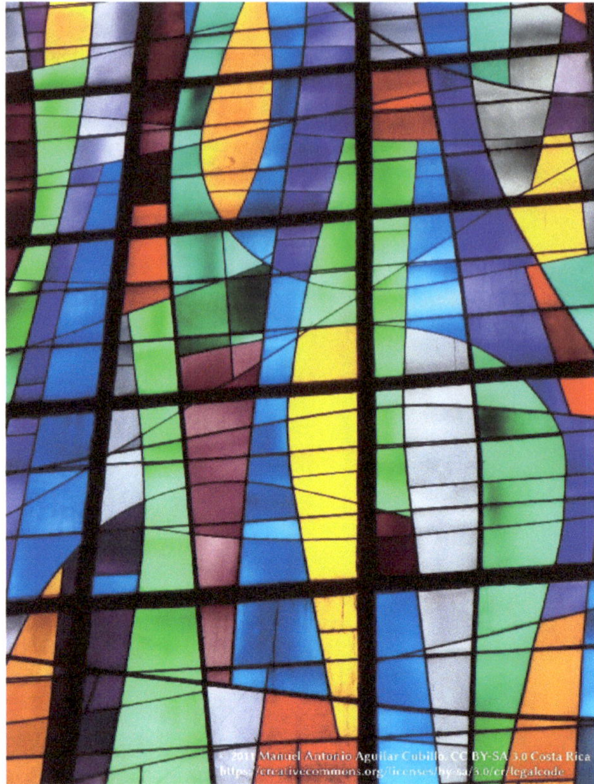

Abstract stained glass window in cathedral of St. Charles Borromeo in Ciudad Quesada. Manuel Antonio Aguilar Cubillo, 2011, Creative Commons

This stained glass window is of an abstract design, found in more modern settings. It comes from the cathedral church of a younger diocese in Costa Rica. The cathedral in San Carlo is more modest than some of the Gothic cathedrals from which some of the other sacred windows featured in this book.

Within the abstract design, you might find traditional symbols that are important to faith. Others view more abstract windows and are simply moved by the interplay of the vibrant colors and the emotions that are created from observing them. This particular window uses different shades of colors as well as a wide spectrum of colors in addition to greys and black.

As you work on this window, what do you see and find in this window? How are you affected by the relative brightness and vibrancy of the coloring of the window? In what ways does modern expressions speak differently about faith than more historic designs of windows?

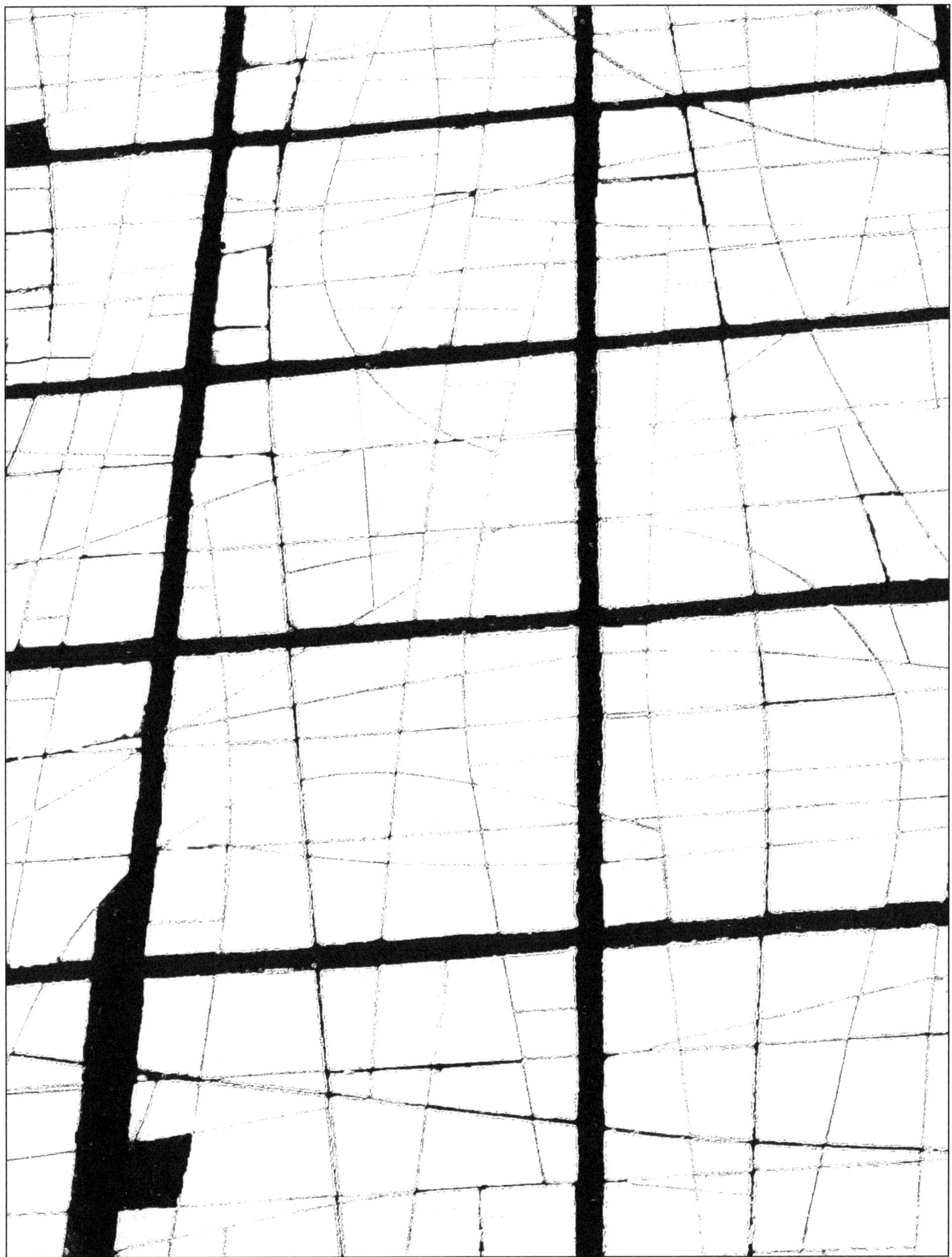

REFLECTION ON COLORING THIS SACRED WINDOW

Use this space to record some of the thoughts from your coloring of this sacred window. These reflections could be about the particular window or be thoughts that you had while coloring.

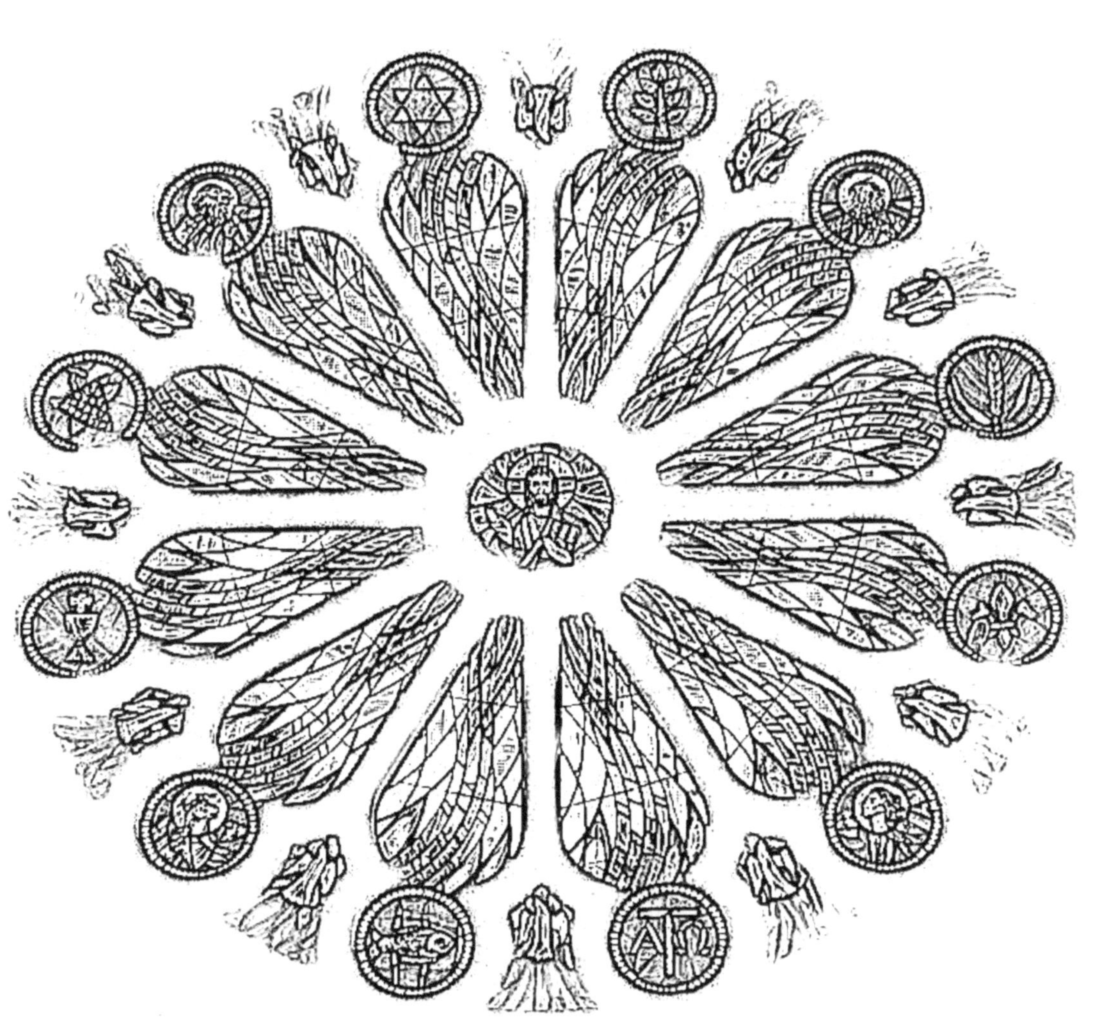

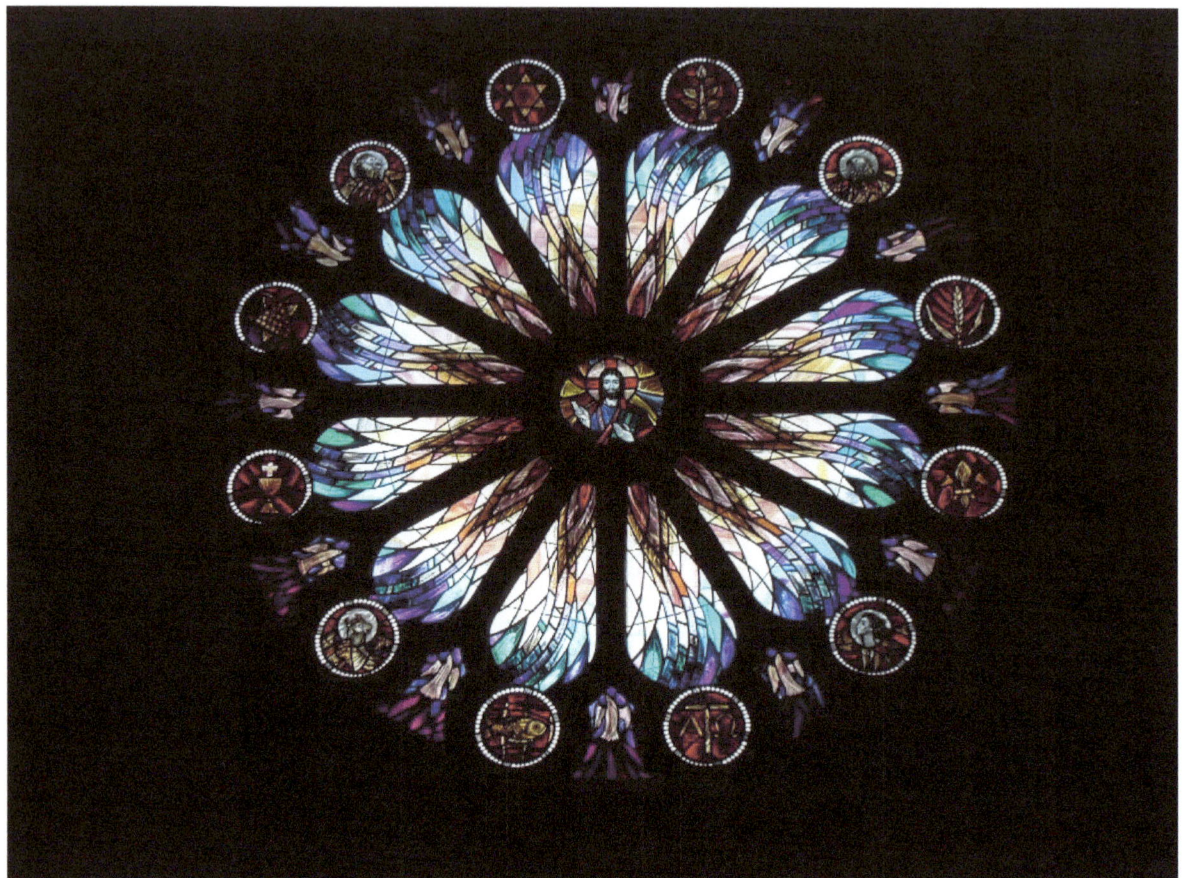

Stained glass window in transept of Christ Church Cathedral, Nelson. Pseudopanax 2011, Public Domain.

This stained glass image comes from a cathedral that was a parish church before it was a diocesean cathedral. In fact, its location, Nelson, only became a city when Queen Victoria named an Anglican diocese after it in 1859. In fact, for thirty years, the church was only the unofficial cathedral of the diocese, only becoming official after being enlarged.

Numerous sites and churches have bore the name of Christ Church in Nelson. The current church began being built in 1925 and was finished in 1965. Along the way, plans were changed given the risks and expense involved in what was the original plans. Because of an earthquake, marble was ground down and mixed with plaster to give it a unique appearance and color.

This stained glass image contains elements that are similar to other rose windows while combining in elements of more modern design. The coloring uses different ranges of colors, including more earth tones in the featherlike spokes. Yet, at the same time, the symbols in the circles use more traditional colors. There is also the repeated pattern of the dove representing the Holy Spirit.

As you work on this set of imagery, you may want to think about how traditional expressions of faith and more modern influences play out in your own understanding of faith. Where are you in continuity with the past and where has the modern world made you adopt things that were not even being considered back then?

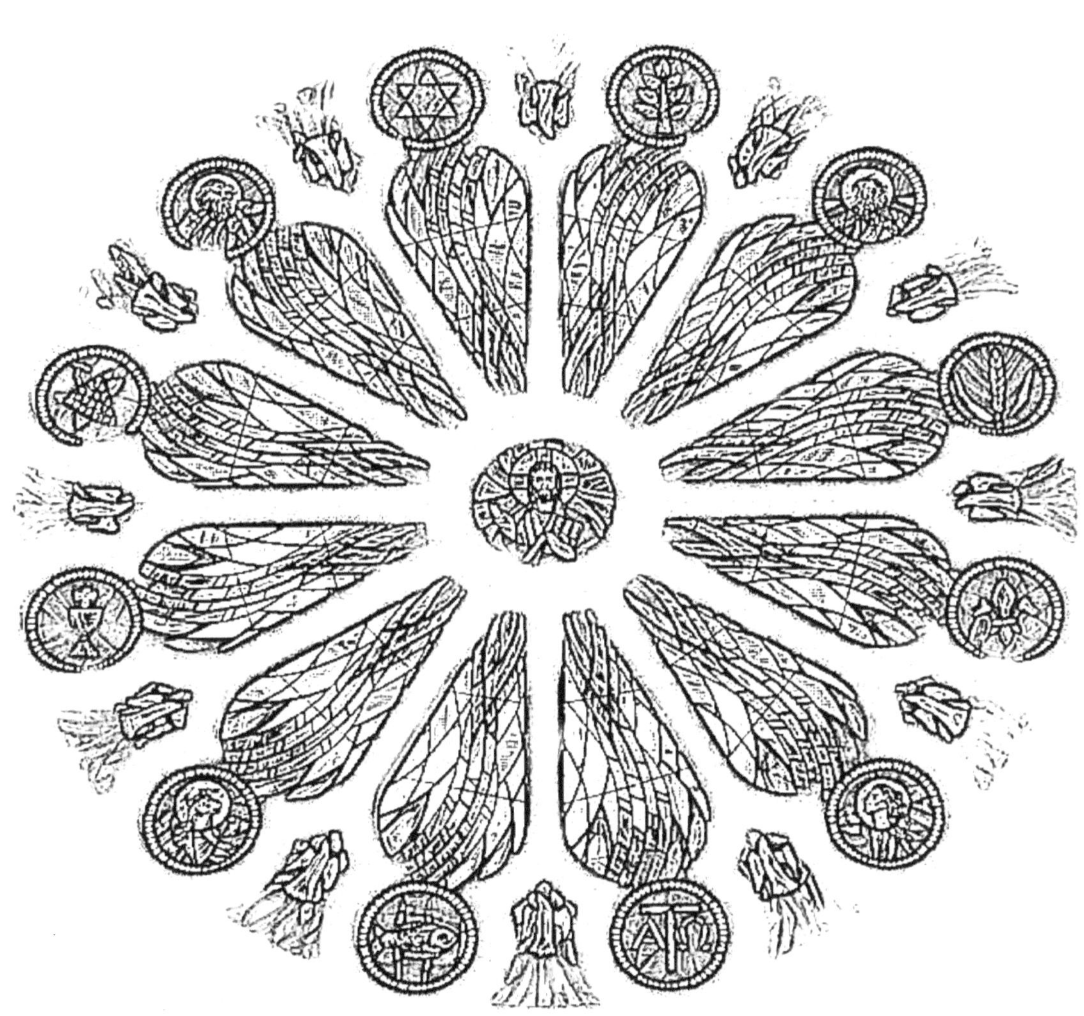

REFLECTION ON COLORING THIS SACRED WINDOW

Use this space to record some of the thoughts from your coloring of this sacred window. These reflections could be about the particular window or be thoughts that you had while coloring.

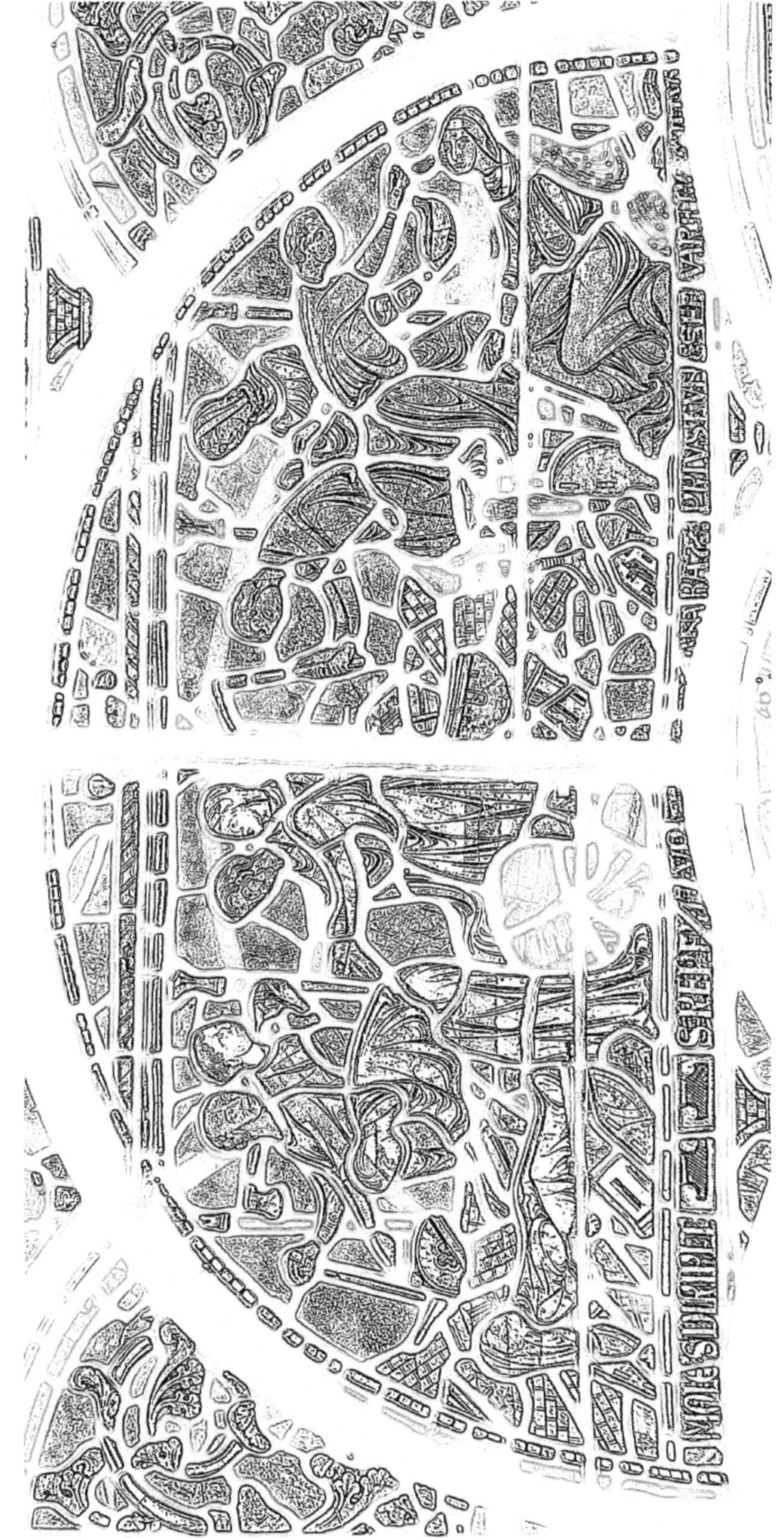

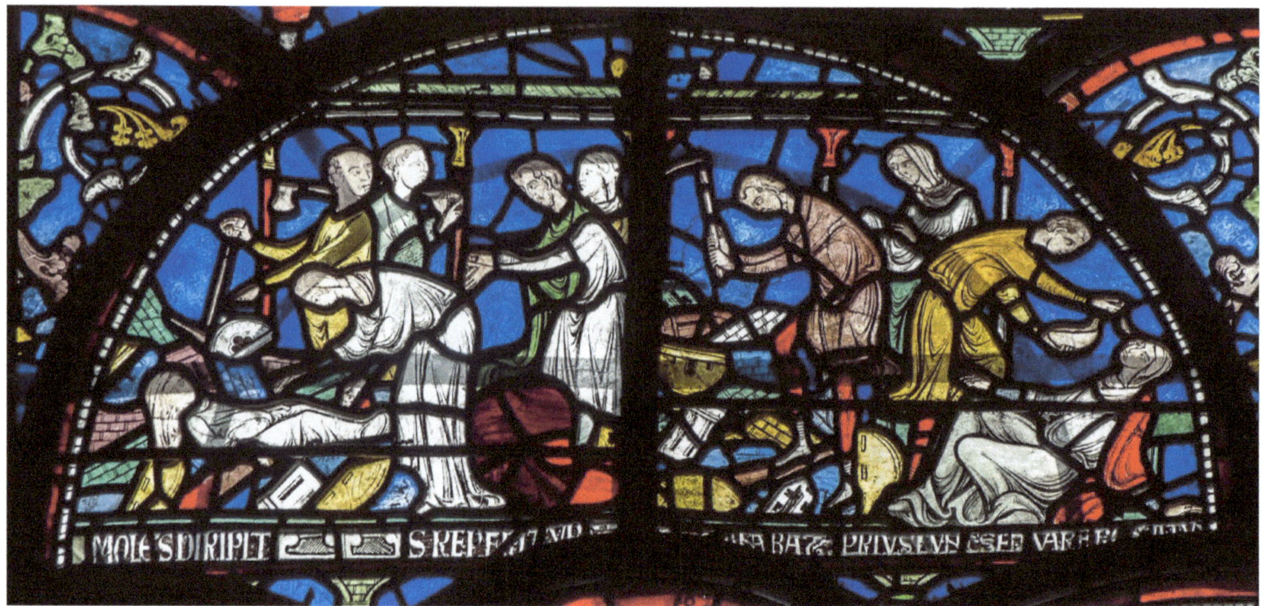

Stained glass windows s.VII, Canterbury Cathedral. Julian P. Guffogg, 2014, Creative Commons.

This window dates back to around 1220, although it has significant amounts of modern glass in its restoration. This window is actually divided into two frames of a story. It is a form of stained glass window that is common and is used to tell a story. This particular example includes text, which is sometimes present in this type of window, although text is also often left off, allowing the picture(s) to tell the story. In older windows (such as this one) the text would have been reserved for more educated viewers, such as the clergy, while the majority of the viewers would obtain the whole story from the images.

This particular window has been called the Cure of Geoffrey of Winchester. It features, in the left panel, the infant Geoffrey being cured by St Thomas from a life threatening illness. Between the left pane and the right pane, it is said that a gale blew down the wall onto his cradle, terrifying his mother (who is having to be revived with water) and grandmother. Meanwhile, others are using tools to clear the debris. The mother cries out to St. Thomas to save her son again. The Latin inscription translates to "The wreckage is torn apart, and the child is found unhurt." This window honors the archbishop that was martyred half a century before this in this cathedral seat that was already six centuries old at this point. Other similar windows tell of Biblical stories.

Canterbury Cathedral is seen as the Mother Church in the Anglican Communion as well as the seat of the Archbishop of Canterbury. It is being included in this collection not only to show the importance of stained glass windows in the broader Christian community but also because Canterbury is a place that many take pilgrimages to.

As you work on this sacred window, what does the story portrayed in it say to you? Does it echo something in your own life? What type of story would you want to memorialize in a window if you were given space in a church near you? Does working on a sacred window that depicts an actual image feel different to you than one that is more geometric?

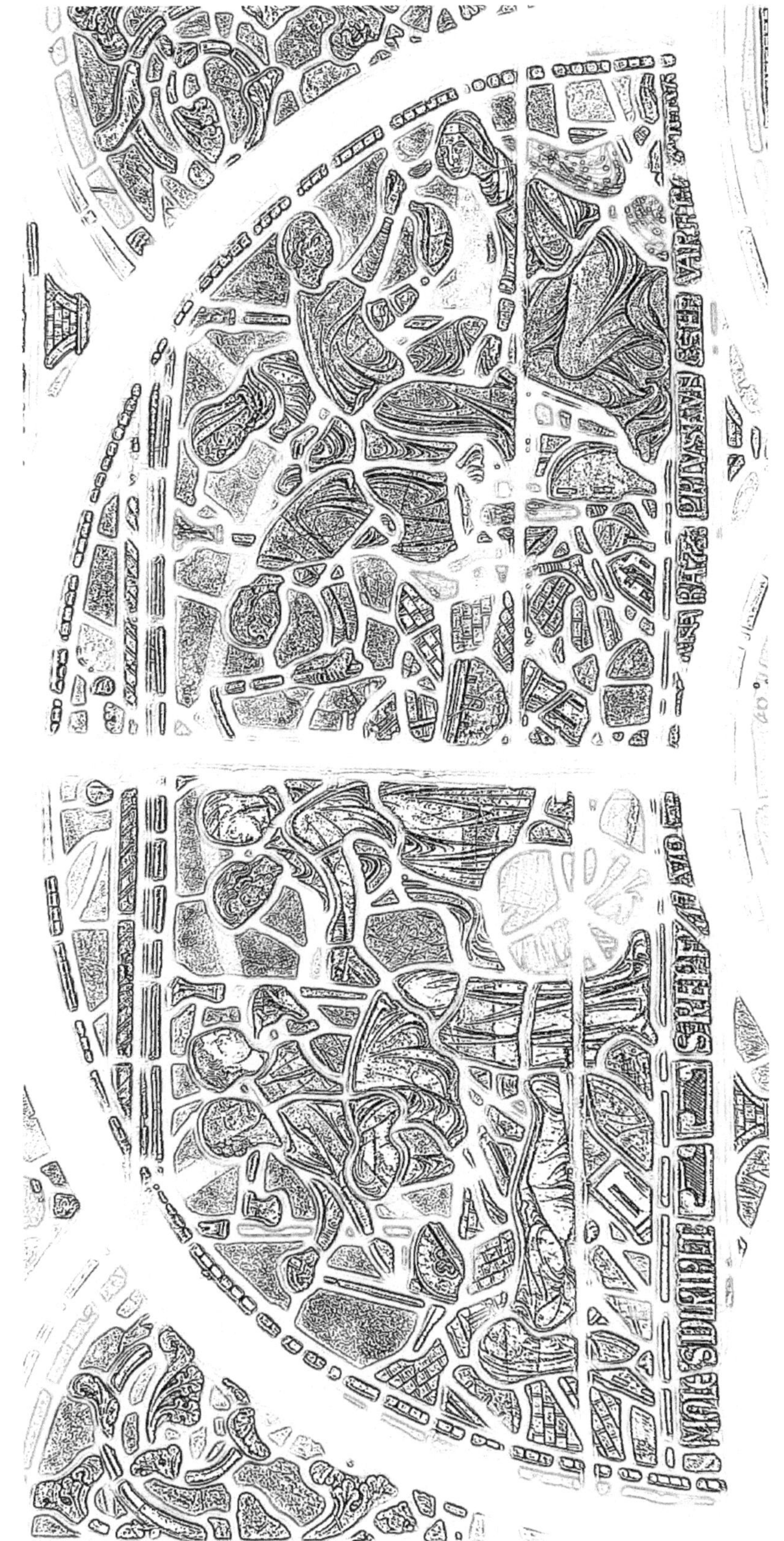

REFLECTION ON COLORING THIS SACRED WINDOW

Use this space to record some of the thoughts from your coloring of this sacred window. These reflections could be about the particular window or be thoughts that you had while coloring.

ABOUT THE AUTHOR

Christopher L. Smith has been involved in a diverse range of areas in terms of his training and experience. However, his approach through life is not to treat these as distinct dimensions, rather to see the connections across various aspects. This book is a good example of that. While studying at Yale Divinity School, he became aware of connections between his training in mathematics (including advanced work in computational geometry) and theological issues, particularly as seen in art and architecture. This background in sacred geometry prompts a different looking at sacred windows that allows him to guide the spiritual development and practice of others.

At the time of preparing this book, Christopher's primary professional work was in the incorporation of spirituality into the therapeutic practice. In so doing, he has walked with people in their spiritual growth in ways that are in addition to his work as a minister and chaplain.

In addition to other books in this Sacred Colors series, Christopher has written on other topics. If you are interested in learning more about his writings, please look him up at http://AnAuthor.com/Christopher.

www.ingramcontent.com/pod-product-compliance
Lightning Source LLC
LaVergne TN
LVHW070156110826
845147LV00002B/424
9780998529509